Careers for Creative People

Careers in Music

Stuart A. Kallen

ReferencePoint Press®

San Diego, CA

© 2020 ReferencePoint Press, Inc.
Printed in the United States

For more information, contact:
ReferencePoint Press, Inc.
PO Box 27779
San Diego, CA 92198
www.ReferencePointPress.com

LIBRARY OF CONGRESS CATALOGING-IN-PUBLICATION DATA

Name: Kallen, Stuart A., 1955– author.
Title: Careers in Music/by Stuart A. Kallen.
Description: San Diego, CA: ReferencePoint Press, [2019] | Series: Careers for Creative People | Audience: Grade 9 to 12. | Includes bibliographical references and index.
Identifiers: LCCN 2019007792 (print) | LCCN 2019007929 (ebook) | ISBN 9781682826843 (eBook) | ISBN 9781682826836 (hardback)
Subjects: LCSH: Music—Vocational guidance—Juvenile literature.
Classification: LCC ML3795 (ebook) | LCC ML3795 .K16 2019 (print) | DDC 780.23—dc23
LC record available at https://lccn.loc.gov/2019007792

Contents

Practice, Listen, and Learn

Someone thinking about a career in music might imagine a disc jockey (DJ) spinning dance tunes to ecstatic crowds at an outdoor festival or a rock star shredding a guitar solo in front of screaming fans in a packed arena. And without a doubt, DJs and rock musicians are some of the most visible examples of people who make a living from music. But millionaire superstars make up only a small percentage of creative people who pursue careers in music.

If the music industry were symbolized by a pyramid, superstars would occupy the lofty territory at the very top. The area below would be inhabited by a larger group who stoke the star-maker machinery, as singer Joni Mitchell put it. This group of professionals—concert promoters, record producers, and talent scouts—combine creative skills with business knowledge.

As the music career pyramid widens, greater numbers of people can be found performing vital services that keep the entertainment industry humming. Musicians and songwriters spend their days playing and composing music and performing in nightclubs and other venues. Professionals who meld a love of music with a passion for science and medicine work as adaptive arts teachers and music therapists. These music lovers heal injuries and promote mental health through singing, strumming, and even banging on drums.

Channel Your Inspiration

If you love music, you can find your place on the music industry pyramid. But making it in the music industry requires more than dreaming of stardom. The most successful people, be they

4

performers, songwriters, or music promoters, understand that the music business is tough and competitive. Those who want to ascend to the top must be diligent, clever, and resourceful. Fortunately, there are solid steps you can take to realize your dreams.

Although it has been said before, it is still worth repeating: you need to practice. Those who are intensely dedicated to perfecting their skills have a far better chance of realizing their desired goals. While practicing can get tedious, another way to channel your inspiration is to formulate a set of realistic career goals. Write them down along with the steps you will take to achieve them. This map for your musical journey will help you stay focused when you need to navigate around the inevitable obstacles that will get in your way.

Superstar singer-songwriter Lady Gaga is an example of someone who knew what she wanted from the start. She told the London *Telegraph* in 2010, "I have always been an artist. And I've always been famous, you just didn't know it yet." Lady Gaga, who began learning piano at age four, played her first gig at fourteen. She thought she was on her way to the top when she got a recording contract with a major record label at age nineteen. But the label quickly dropped her. Gaga worked through the disappointment by writing songs, performing with a rock band, and learning all she could about fashion and dance. For a time, Lady Gaga worked behind the scenes writing hits for New Kids on the Block and rhythm-and-blues singer Akon. But her original goal was to attain the success she knew was her destiny. Lady Gaga's ambitions were realized in 2008 with the release of her best-selling album fittingly titled *Fame*.

Most people will never be the next Lady Gaga (or Taylor Swift or Bruno Mars or Kanye West). But those who want a work life that revolves around music can build success the way Gaga did—by practicing, listening, and learning. But success requires a skill that is harder to learn. The music industry thrives on personal relationships. While developing the right contacts is easier for some than others, it is an essential skill in an industry where making connections with peers and professionals is crucial.

Careers in Music

Occupation	Job Description	Pay Range
DJ	Club DJs play songs at a nightclub, bar, rave, or party using vinyl records, CDs, or MP3s.	$500 to $1,000+ per night
Songwriter	Songwriters craft songs for another artist in hopes of creating a hit.	$0–$1,000,000+
Jingle Writer	Jingle writers write music for commercials.	$500 to $15,000+ per commercial
A&R Administrator	A&R administrators find fresh talent for a label and oversee the completion of new albums.	$27,000 to $85,000+
Concert Promoter	Concert promoters organize shows by booking talent, securing venues, and marketing their events.	$0 to $1,000,000+
Tour Manager	Tour managers plan and organize transportation, scheduling, and the financial aspects of an artist's time on the road.	$25,000–$125,000
Music Journalist	Music journalists write music criticism and music news for print, online, and broadcast media.	$15,000–$30,000+
Music Teacher	Music teachers instruct students in performance and music theory and lead various performance ensembles.	$30,000–$71,200
Publicist	Publicists create press kits, write press releases, and contact media to secure coverage for artists and albums.	$25,000 to $150,000+
Conductor	Conductors lead orchestras, operas, and other musical ensembles during live performances.	$15,000 to $275,000+
Choir Director	Choir directors coordinate choirs, recruit singers, develop and train musical talents, and select music for performances.	$20,000 to $42,000
Music Therapist	Music therapists use music to help clients overcome and manage emotional, physical, cognitive, and social difficulties.	$20,000 to $135,000
Instrument Sales Rep	Instrument sales reps visit musical instrument retail stores in their territory to sell instruments and sound gear.	$19,000 to $75,000+
Instrument Repairer	Instrument repairers fix and restore broken or neglected musical instruments.	$9 to $55+ an hour
Choreographer	Choreographers create dances and teach them to dancers who perform them during concert tours and theatrical performances and for film or TV projects.	$20,000–$81,000
Cruise Ship Entertainer	Cruise ship entertainers perform a wide variety of music to entertain guests on board cruise ships.	$24,000–$54,000+

Source: Careers in Music. www.careersinmusic.com.

Whether you hope to become a musical superstar, a music publicist, a video game sound designer, or a choreographer, passion and commitment are necessary for success. Chances are you would make more money as an investment banker or a software engineer, but living a life surrounded by music has its own rewards, as composer and performer Greg Moore writes on the website Quora: "[Musicians] have a stronger desire to make music than to make money. The music is always playing in their heads—it needs to be released and set free to beautify the world."

Songwriter

In 1989, when Heather Morgan was just five years old, she began stringing words together to form song lyrics. By the time she was in her late twenties, Morgan was working as a staff writer for the music publishing division of a major Nashville music label. She excelled at her craft and went on to write hit songs for country superstars like Brett Eldredge, Dierks Bentley, Keith Urban, and Maddie & Tae.

As a songwriter, Morgan dedicates her life to expressing compelling musical stories. She writes melodies, rhythms, and musical "hooks" meant to grab the attention of the listener. Some of her lyrics are simple and to the point; others contain sweeping, cinematic poetry. In an interview with *American Songwriter* magazine, Morgan describes how these elements come together: "[My song 'We Were a Fire'] encompassed so many things I wanted to have in a song. . . . It captured a real experience; there was an edge to the instrumentation; the writing had imagery and metaphor; and the melody had range and pop sensibility."

At a Glance

Songwriter

Minimum Educational Requirements
Degree not required, but training in music theory and composition is helpful

Personal Qualities
Hardworking; determined; creative; ability to accept rejection; strong belief in yourself and your talents

Working Conditions
Irregular hours in rehearsal studios, recording studios, and live music venues

Salary
$50,590 annual median income in 2017*

Number of Jobs
74,800 in 2017

Future Job Outlook
6 percent growth through 2026*

*Includes songwriters and composers

Contrary to what the term *staff writer* implies, songwriters like Morgan are not employees, nor are they staff members, at a music publishing company. Staff writers sign exclusive songwriting contracts granting music publishers the rights to sell their songs. In return for this commitment, staff writers receive royalties—a percentage of the money generated by sales of the songs they write.

Staff writing contracts contain what is called a delivery requirement; this spells out the specific number of songs the writer must produce annually. The delivery requirement is usually ten to fifteen songs. If a staff writer cowrites with another staff writer, each songwriter receives half a credit toward their delivery requirement. If a staff writer cowrites with two people, one-third credit is given to each. Since staff writers often collaborate with others, they usually work on anywhere from fifteen to thirty songs per year to meet their delivery requirements.

Like any good songwriter, Morgan draws from her personal experiences. She wrote the song "Your Hurricane" after an emotional breakup with her boyfriend. On the *American Songwriter* website, Morgan describes how she wrote the song: "I sang that chorus idea till I had it, and then, I sang verse line ideas over and over again. I was living in the emotion of that song at the time, so I was also making sure the lyrics lined up with the heartache I was feeling. Capturing emotion is really important to me."

Songwriting is one of the few jobs where employers expect employees to reveal their innermost thoughts, dreams, fantasies, and sentiments. But this is only part of the job. Songwriters work closely with artists and repertoire (A&R) managers at record companies. A&R folks set up recording sessions where songwriters record demonstration recordings, or demos, of a song. Demos are usually simple recordings that consist of a single instrument and vocal supplied by the songwriter. If the song is more complex, a demo might include a band or even a full orchestra. However, music publishers require songwriters to pay for the studio time and the backing musicians used on a demo. This can cost thousands of dollars, so most staff writers keep things simple. Once a demo is finished, A&R managers try to find interested recording artists, producers, and other song buyers—a task known as shopping or pitching the demo.

There are many benefits to being a staff writer, and numerous people are competing for a small number of openings. This leaves many dedicated songwriters to work as freelancers. They write songs, create demos, and play their music in clubs, theaters, and other venues. This type of work requires passion and dedication. Performing songwriters must constantly promote their music on social media and reach out to record producers and A&R managers while touring to pay their bills.

How Do You Become a Songwriter?

Education

A college degree is not necessary for aspiring songwriters, as staff writer Jason Blume says on CareersInMusic.com: "Music publishers don't care whether or not you have a degree in songwriting, or what else you've done. It's a business, and they care about one thing: whether you can deliver songs that they believe will earn you—and them—lots of money."

Most songwriters who make a lot of money for themselves and their publishers say they began making up songs when they were very young. And some find success at an early age. Taylor Swift was only fourteen when she was signed as a staff writer by the Nashville branch of Sony/ATV Music Publishing. However, most aspiring songwriters are not as naturally talented—or as lucky—as Taylor Swift. They need to develop their songwriting skills by studying music, poetry, and recording techniques.

Almost every songwriter is a skilled musician who knows how to play guitar, piano, or another instrument. Playing music helps a songwriter develop an understanding of melody, harmony, rhythm, and music theory. Some musicians are self-taught, but others take music lessons. Despite Blume's observation, some songwriters go to college and earn a bachelor's degree in musical composition or theory.

Smart songwriters also take the time to learn as much as possible about the music industry's business practices. Record companies and music publishers are notorious for taking advantage of people who do not understand the complex legalities of songwriting credits, copyrights, licensing, and royalties. While successful songwriters hire lawyers and managers to deal with these issues, educated songwriters can protect their own interests.

Skills and Personality

Songwriter Evan Zwisler writes on the *Bandzoogle Blog,* "If you're a songwriter, you're not simply playing music, you're imbuing our lives with a soundtrack that is evocative, thought provoking, and deeply meaningful." This requires songwriters to be creative, to be able to look inside themselves, and to find inspiration and emotions that can be translated into lyrics and music. But musical vision does not always appear on command. Many songwriters are voracious readers who find inspiration in books of poetry, art, music, and history. Some watch old movies to pick out dialogue; others take inspiration from novels or magazines and newspapers.

Most professional songwriters will say that creativity and inspiration are only part of the job. As Blume explains, the job requires a strong work ethic:

> I had a fantasy that songwriters lay out by their pool, sipping a drink, and waiting for a brilliant song to strike them. HA! The successful writers I know work incredibly long hours. When they're not busy writing songs, they're doing demos, having business meetings, and hanging out with people who can advance their careers. . . . The successful songwriters I know are driven and are almost always either working—or thinking about their work.

As with any job in the arts, songwriters must have a strong belief in their own talents. This provides a cushion for the rejection songwriters will inevitably face when a tune they have spent many hours creating is rejected.

A songwriter ponders the words and music that will express a compelling musical story. Once the song is written, songwriters make demo recordings as a first step toward finding interested recording artists or other song buyers.

On the Job

Employers

Staff writers usually sign a five-year contract with a record label's music publishing division. Most major pop, rock, and hip-hop record labels are located in New York City and Los Angeles. Nashville is the center of the country music scene. While it is not a requirement, most staff writers live where publishers are located because it allows them to interact on a daily basis with producers, agents, musicians, and other songwriters.

Wherever music publishers might be located, they are in the song business. They take the songs written by staff writers and sell the tunes to recording artists, and producers of films, television shows, and commercials. Once a song is sold the music publisher collects the money generated worldwide by downloads, streaming, compact disc sales, live performances, and other uses of the work. The A&R staff at a music publishing company works to promote its staff writers. They show a staff writer's work to producers of specific projects or pair the songwriter with recording artists or other successful songwriters. Songwriters who work with well-known artists have a much greater chance of getting their music on a record and thus generating royalties.

Working Conditions

Since staff writers are not employees, most work from home studios or small offices with areas set aside for rehearsing, performing, and recording. Staff writers work their own hours and write when inspiration hits, whether it is at four o'clock in the afternoon or four o'clock in the morning.

Most staff writers enhance their income by performing solo or with bands in bars and nightclubs. While a struggling songwriter might see this as a dream job, there are shortcomings. Staff writers, like freelance songwriters, do not receive any fringe benefits such as health insurance or retirement plans.

Earnings

Songwriters earn a living from royalties, whether they are staff writers or freelancers. Those who are staff writers are often paid an advance. This is money the staff writer is paid against future royalties; once royalties start coming in, the publisher keeps all moneys until the advance is paid back. Then the staff writer starts getting paid.

Staff writers just starting out, who have not shown they can generate profits for a music publisher, can expect an advance of $15,000 to $35,000 a year. Those who work in Nashville, which has a lower cost of living, are paid less than staff writers in New York City and Los Angeles. Staff writers who do not receive a large advance often work part-time jobs to survive. Successful staff writers who have written a number of hit records can receive advances exceeding $200,000 a year.

The US Bureau of Labor Statistics (BLS) reports that the median income for a songwriter in 2017 was $50,590. However, this is one career with an extreme difference between those who earn the most and those who earn the least. Although some staff writers never earn a dollar, those who consistently write for superstars make millions of dollars in royalties every year. For example, Swedish songwriter Max Martin, who is hardly a household name, has earned over $250 million working behind the scenes writing hits for The Weeknd, Katy Perry, Maroon 5, and others.

Opportunities for Advancement

Numerous successful staff writers are able to use their industry connections to make a name for themselves as major stars in their own right. This is especially true in Nashville, where superstars from Dolly Parton to Sam Hunt, Kasey Musgraves, and Chris Stapleton began their careers as staff writers. Even those who do not pursue solo careers can do very well if they write the hits that the public loves.

What Is the Future Outlook for Songwriters?

According to the BLS, employment for songwriters and composers is expected to grow by 6 percent through 2026. The bureau expects film, television, and commercials to generate the greatest demand.

Find Out More

American Society of Composers, Authors and Publishers (ASCAP)
250 W. Fifty-Seventh St.
New York, NY 10107
website: www.ascap.com

ASCAP is a performance rights organization that protects the musical copyrights of its members and pays royalties when a song is broadcast or played live. The ASCAP Foundation funds music education, talent development, humanitarian programs, and offers scholarships to students at all levels.

Broadcast Music Inc. (BMI)
7 World Trade Ctr.
250 Greenwich St.
New York, NY 10007
website: www.bmi.com

BMI is a performance rights organization that collects fees on behalf of songwriters, composers, and music publishers in all genres. The BMI Foundation offers scholarships, internships, and awards to aspiring songwriters, video game composers, and radio broadcasters.

Nashville Songwriters Association International (NSAI)
1710 Roy Acuff Pl.
Nashville, TN 37203
website: www.nashvillesongwriters.com

The NSAI is the world's biggest songwriter trade association. It provides members with information about legal issues, workshop opportunities, and help with song pitches. The NSAI annual song contest is open to anyone thirteen years of age and older, and prizes include money, professional mentoring sessions, and songwriting contracts.

National Association of Schools of Music (NASM)
11250 Roger Bacon Dr., Suite 21
Reston, VA 20190
website: https://nasm.arts-accredit.org

Nearly 650 accredited conservatories, music schools, universities, and colleges belong to the National Association of Schools of Music, which establishes national standards for music degrees and credentials. The "Student and Parents" link on the NASM website provides information about music programs, financial aid, and grants and scholarships.

Adaptive Arts Teacher

What Does an Adaptive Arts Teacher Do?

"Artists come in all shapes, sizes and abilities," says adaptive arts teacher Jetta Cruse. The appreciation for artists of all skill levels inspired Cruse to found the Michiana Performing and Adaptive Arts Community (MPAAAC) in South Bend, Indiana. The MPAAAC is a performing arts school attended by fifty musicians, singers, dancers, and other performers who have neurological differences that result in autism, Asperger's syndrome, and attention-deficit/hyperactivity disorder (ADHD).

Cruse began her career as a performing artist who toured with a children's musical act, Jetta and the Jellybeans, for more than a decade. During her travels, Cruse met differently abled children whose musical talents were not being nurtured. This led her to establish the MPAAAC in 2016. Cruse described her students to the *South Bend Tribune* in 2018: "They're viable performing artists that have the ability to play great music, the ability to express themselves. So I just made it my mission that I'm going to move heaven and earth to change the

At a Glance

Adaptive Arts Teacher

Minimum Educational Requirements
Bachelor of education or bachelor of art degree

Personal Qualities
Teaching skills; patience; good communicator; empathy for special needs community

Certification and Licensing
Public school teachers need to be licensed and certified

Working Conditions
Part- or full-time teaching in classrooms, art studios, theaters, and rehearsal spaces

Salary
$54,000 in 2017*

Number of Jobs
95,110 in 2017*

Future Job Outlook
6 percent through 2024*

*Includes all art teachers

community's mind about people with different abilities." As part of this process, Cruse and her students produce a Christmas showcase, which plays to a packed house every year at a local music venue.

Adaptive arts teachers like Cruse understand that playing music, dancing, acting, drawing, painting, and sculpting can bring a sense of joy to the creator. And making art and music can also provide a profound sense of satisfaction to those whose creative urges have not always been encouraged. As adaptive arts specialist Susan D. Loesl explains in a guide published by Washington, DC's Kennedy Center for the Performing Arts, "The lives of students who have experienced adaptive art making have been changed in ways that others may not understand. As with most students, the experience of art making is very personal. . . . The work that is created comes from the very essence of who they are. Two plus two does not have to equal four and painting outside of the lines is celebrated."

Creating art can be therapeutic, but adaptive arts teachers are not trained art therapists. Art therapy is a mental health profession practiced by those who are trained in psychology, behavioral disorders, and therapeutic techniques. The role of the adaptive arts teacher is to help differently abled students expand their artistic abilities, not analyze their problems. Adaptive arts teachers design activities to promote fundamental abilities in a range of art forms. They help students improve their self-expression, social interaction, and group participation skills.

Adaptive arts teachers use their training to adapt the tools of art making, from paint brushes to ukuleles, so that they may be used by those whose bodies work differently. For example, some of Cruse's performers find it difficult to place their fingers on guitar strings to form basic chords. These students learn to hold the guitars flat on their laps and play chords with metal slide bars like those commonly used by blues guitar players. And the goal is not about performing a flawless song or dance routine but providing pathways for students to express themselves in a nonjudgmental atmosphere.

Adaptive arts teachers determine the needs of each individual student in order to provide them with appropriate instruction. Schools like the College of Adaptive Arts in San Jose, California, provide courses that offer a wide range of interesting subjects to students with special needs. For example, the college provides postsecondary students with classes in dance, television and film production, art, music, and theater. Courses provide instruction in ballet, folk dance, digital music production, singing, and songwriting.

How Do You Become an Adaptive Arts Teacher?

Education

Adaptive arts teachers who wish to work for public schools need to have a bachelor's degree in education or special education. Prospective adaptive arts teachers should consider majoring in education while pursuing a minor in art, music, dance, or theater, depending on their artistic talents. Coursework in a teacher education program includes studies in child and adolescent development, lesson preparation, and teaching diverse learners. Those interested in pursuing a career in adaptive arts should take courses in psychology along with classes that focus on strategies for teaching children with exceptional educational needs.

Many public schools only hire teachers who hold master's degrees in the subjects they teach. For example, biology teachers have a master's in biology. Those who wish to pursue a career as an adaptive arts teacher should consider getting a master's degree in performing arts. These degree programs combine classroom studies with classes that may include music ensembles, audition techniques, and stage performance. Theater students study stage movements, choreography, acting styles, dance techniques, playwriting, and directing. Music students concentrate on music theory, composition, performance, voice, and music history and analysis.

Degreed art teachers interested in additional training in adaptive arts education can attend adaptive arts workshops and seminars like those offered by the international organization on arts and the differently abled known as the VSA (formerly known as the Very Special Arts). The VSA, which is sponsored by the Kennedy Center, holds regular seminars throughout the country.

Certification and Licensing

All teaching jobs in public schools require certification. However, many private schools and other educational institutions do not require certification. While requirements vary from state to state, most require applicants to complete a teacher preparation program and pass a teacher certification test. Teachers are also required to pass a background check that typically includes inspection of local, state, and federal crime records; driving records; and credit scores.

The National Association of Special Education Teachers offers board certification in special education. This accreditation does not replace state licensing, but it is available to those who wish to demonstrate their commitment to excellence to employers, administrators, parents, and students.

Volunteer Work and Internships

The adaptive arts community relies on volunteers, and prospective adaptive arts teachers can learn by donating their time. At Westfield High School in Fairfax County, Virginia, for example, college students are encouraged to volunteer as teaching assistants in adaptive arts classes. And these students can learn a lot even as they help others. In a Fairfax County Public Schools documentary about the class, a volunteer named Gloria explained, "I've built friendships. I sit with kids [I work with] every day at lunch now. Socially it has helped me so much and then it's also given me the confidence to go into special education as a career knowing that I am passionate about it and have . . . the basic skills I need to go into it."

Skills and Personality

Adaptive arts teachers must have a sincere desire to work with, and understand, students with a wide range of conditions. Most students in adaptive arts classes have neurodiversity issues. John Elder Robison, the author of an autobiography about living with Asperger's, defines the term *neurodiversity* in *Psychology Today*: "Neurodiversity is the idea that neurological differences like autism and ADHD are the result of normal, natural variation in the human genome. This represents a new and fundamentally different way of looking at conditions that were traditionally [thought of as] disease or injury."

While all teachers need patience, resourcefulness, empathy, and good communication skills, these traits are especially important for adaptive arts teachers. Compassion is a necessary quality for those who work with students who express themselves differently or who require instructions to be repeated or communicated slowly. Adaptive arts teachers also need to communicate skillfully with parents and caregivers. Interpersonal skills are important because adaptive arts teachers are required to build strong personal relationships with other teachers, school counselors, doctors, and psychologists. Adaptive arts teachers also need to be resourceful when presenting new concepts and activities to those who learn differently than others.

On the Job

Employers

Adaptive arts teachers are often employed as traditional art, music, or drama teachers in public schools. If a school has a large population of students with special education needs, an adaptive arts teacher might work solely with these kids in a self-contained class. In schools with fewer special needs students, adaptive arts specialists might coteach with regular art or music teachers. In some cases, an adaptive arts teacher will work several days a week, visiting multiple schools within a district on a regular schedule. Part-time teachers might fill in their free time teaching classes at private studios, private schools, or community arts and after-school programs, or they might work with special needs service providers.

Working Conditions

Adaptive arts teachers work in classrooms, art studios, theaters, and rehearsal spaces. Some work part-time at several institutions; others are employed full-time, which can require them to work more than forty hours a week. Teachers who work in public schools often have a two- to three-month break during the summer, along with short holiday and midwinter breaks. Those who visit multiple schools are required to commute locally using their personal vehicles or public transportation.

Earnings

In 2017 the median salary for all music, art, and drama instructors in high school was $55,000. Elementary school teachers were paid less, around $53,000.

Opportunities for Advancement

Many adaptive arts teachers begin their careers as regular art teachers and go on to open their own private studios or take jobs with private schools or community institutions. Some adaptive arts teachers like Cruse establish their own nonprofits dedicated to special needs students. Most teachers who work in this field are not driven by career advancement or wages. They are dedicated to serving their communities and empowering individuals with different abilities.

What Is the Future Outlook for Adaptive Arts Teachers?

Adaptive arts teaching is a relatively new profession that has only been considered a specialty since the middle of the first decade of the 2000s. However, there are over 6.6 million students with special needs in the United States, prompting Loesl to comment that there are "too many students, too few art specialists." While the number of adaptive arts teachers is expected to grow in the coming years, there are no specific figures for the profession. The US Bureau of Labor Statistics estimates that the demand for primary and secondary school art, music, and drama teachers will grow by 6 percent through 2024.

Find Out More

College of Adaptive Arts
1401 Parkmoor Ave.
San Jose, CA 95126
website: www.collegeofadaptivearts.org

This school was founded in 2009 to provide a postsecondary education to adults with special needs who have not traditionally had access to a college education. Students interested in teaching adaptive arts can find information about various programs provided by the college.

National Association of Private Special Education Centers (NAPSEC)
601 Pennsylvania Ave. NW
Washington, DC 20004
website: www.napsec.org

This association provides programs for preschool, elementary, and secondary school students and adults with mild to severe disabilities in over sixty different categories. The NAPSEC website offers accreditation services and lists job openings at private special education programs.

National Association of Special Education Teachers (NASET)
1250 Connecticut Ave. NW
Washington, DC 20036
website: www.naset.org

This professional organization supports and assists those who teach in the area of special education. The NASET website contains professional resources, including a video library, certification requirements, and a library with numerous publications.

Upstream Arts
3501 Chicago Ave. S.
Minneapolis, MN 55407
website: www.upstreamarts.org

Upstream Arts provides adaptive arts services to individuals with special needs. The organization's website features articles, studies, and other educational resources to anyone interested in adaptive arts education.

VSA
2700 F St. NW
Washington, DC 20566
website: www.education.kennedy-center.org/education/vsa

The VSA, once known as the Very Special Arts, is affiliated with the Kennedy Center for the Performing Arts. The VSA website offers numerous resources for adaptive arts teachers and students with special needs, including links to VSA programs, adaptive tools, and advocacy organizations.

Musician

What Does a Musician Do?

In 1966 the popular rock band Lovin' Spoonful had a hit song called "Nashville Cats." The lyrics painted a playful picture of the high-quality, but largely unknown, Nashville session musicians (cats) who backed up the country music stars of the day. More than half a century later, cats in Nashville continue to work behind the scenes, playing on records by country's biggest stars. These guitarists, bassists, fiddlers, vocalists, drummers, and others play on records and live in concert with superstars like Keith Urban, Jessica Simpson, Blake Shelton, and many others.

While Nashville is the country music capital of the world, the talented session musicians who work there are not limited by style. Most are influenced by rock, jazz, pop, blues, and rhythm-and-blues (R&B) musicians. Grant Mickelson, who sings and plays guitar, is a good example of a successful session musician. He was born and raised in Iowa and taught himself to play in sixth grade. He learned to imitate guitar heroes like Eddy Van Halen and Stevie Ray Vaughn,

At a Glance

Musician

Minimum Educational Requirements
Degree not required, but training in music theory and composition is helpful

Personal Qualities
Talent; dedication to music; good communication skills; ability to accept criticism and rejection; physical strength

Working Conditions
Late nights and weekends in bars, concert halls, and reception halls

Pay
$27 an hour in 2017

Number of Jobs
172,400 in 2016

Future Job Outlook
6 percent growth through 2016

which led him to take music lessons in high school and major in music in college.

Mickelson loved rock music but felt that, with his talents, he had a better chance of making a living as a country musician in Nashville. He began his career in 2004 playing in various bands that performed in the honky-tonk bars in downtown Nashville. In 2005, after auditioning for country singer Sara Evans—three times—Mickelson was hired for her backup band. He lasted two weeks before being fired for being too inexperienced. The guitarist struggled for several years, working minimum-wage jobs. He got his big break in 2007, when he was asked to join the Agency, Taylor Swift's backup band. During the eight years that followed, Mickelson played hundreds of concerts with Swift. He played acoustic guitar and mandolin and occasionally shared a microphone with Swift as a harmony vocalist.

Mickelson is one of many working musicians who calls himself a "hired gun." He acknowledges that there are hundreds of better guitarists in Nashville. But as Mickelson told the Behind the Setlist website in 2017, you do not have to be the best to land a great gig (job): "You obviously have to be able to solo and do lots of other things, but if you go into a gig and you're just solid, that's going to be successful, I guarantee it. . . . A lot of people over-play and they don't get the gig because they can't just stop and play the song the way it's supposed to be."

Mickelson earned a six-figure salary while working with Swift, making him one of the more successful musicians whose name most people do not know. After the gig ended, like many Nashville pickers, Mickelson had to pursue other sources of revenue. He earns income playing gigs in clubs and touring with lesser-known acts. Like many hired guns, Mickelson teaches guitar and works with a songwriting partner to create original music. He also does session work, laying down guitar tracks in recording studios for clients who pay by the hour for his expertise. Online recording sessions provide another source of income. Musicians send Mickelson digital copies of their songs and he adds his guitar to the mix. During these sessions, he works with clients using video chat, text, and e-mail.

Musicians practice together before a performance. Many musicians act as their own agents, managers, and record producers; they secure gigs, read contracts, and make audio files for promotion, sales, and social media posts.

Mickelson achieved his status as an in-demand session musician through hard work and countless hours of practice. Professional musicians train their vocal cords and (depending on the instrument) the muscles of the fingers, hands, arms, legs, and lips to play their instruments accurately and expertly. Musicians with good muscle control can concentrate on the inspirational aspects of music—providing a soulful connection between the player and the listener. But as the well-known quote from rock singer Van Morrison makes clear, "Music is spiritual. The music business is not." People who earn a living playing music need to worry about nonspiritual business functions like marketing, booking, promotion, and accounting.

Most musicians act as their own agents, managers, and record producers. In the role of agent, they contact bars, clubs, event planners, and booking agents to book gigs. While working to manage their careers, musicians secure gigs and read contracts to ensure they are getting a fair deal. Musicians who have their own bands must also manage money, paying themselves and other band members, maintaining equipment, and budgeting for transportation, food, and accommodations. Musicians must also learn the art of recording so they can make audio files for promotion, sales, and social media posts. This requires developing the technical skills to handle recording equipment, computers, and music apps.

Industry experts recommend that independent musicians spend half their time working on music and the other half on the business of music. And sometimes the business aspect can take up more than half of a musician's time. As music publicist Ariel Hyatt explains on the Musician Think Tank website, "A successful music career involves spending a large part of your day on non-musical tasks [including] curating social media content, updating your website, booking performances/scheduling with musicians, researching venues, music blogs, music services, [and] promoting your performances."

How Do You Become a Musician?

Education

There are no educational requirements for becoming a musician. Some of the world's most famous musicians are self-taught. Some of music's biggest superstars, including Taylor Swift, David Bowie, Prince, and Jimi Hendrix, never attended music classes, and some cannot even read music. However, most session musicians, as well as those who perform with choirs and symphony orchestras, need to be skilled at sight-reading music. This means they can play a song for the first time by reading its musical notation.

Most music students who take band class in middle or high school learn to sight-read. This skill is necessary for college-bound students who wish to pursue a bachelor of music degree. Those who engage in this intensive four-year program study music theory and analysis, music history, and composition. These music classes take up two-thirds to three-quarters of a student's time. Music schools offering bachelor of music degrees also require students to take four years of instrument lessons, culminating in recitals in junior and senior years.

Many experienced players note that there are pros and cons to pursuing a music degree. On the negative side, classes often focus extensively on the technical aspects of playing while ignoring artistic intangibles like creative inspiration. But there are many advantages of having a music education, as music teacher Keith Ziemba explained on the Quora website in 2018: "The critical thinking skills, the concentration, the idea of working toward a group goal, increased abilities in math, discipline, and personal achievement are all by-products of a music education."

Volunteer Work and Internships

Most musicians feel that any gig is better than no gig, and even professionals play for little or no money at many points in their careers. Musicians volunteer to play at school dances, private parties, street fairs, and other social events. These gigs help a player gain experience in front of an audience while (hopefully) building up a fan base. Musicians often use pictures and videos from nonpaying jobs to promote themselves on social media and provide demos (demonstration recordings) for managers and booking agents.

Skills and Personality

There is an old saying that the only thing a rock guitarist needs is three chords and an attitude. But musicians need more than attitude. They must be dedicated to their art. They often have to prove their skills in auditions and force a smile when they are rejected. Musicians also need the self-discipline necessary for spending hours practicing.

Musicians are also team players who need to cooperate with other musicians as well as conductors, managers, producers, recording techs, and others. Musicians need to be able to communicate clearly and gracefully accept constructive criticism. Business skills are important for those who promote their performances online and in their community. And, as anyone who has ever played music professionally will tell you, a musician needs physical strength. Musicians often travel extensively, keep irregular hours, transport and set up heavy sound equipment, and move around on stage for hours while holding an instrument.

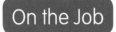

On the Job

Employers

Musicians play everywhere live music is heard, from coffeehouses to Super Bowl halftime shows. Those who play rock, pop, country, blues, R&B, and jazz make their living in bars and nightclubs, and classical musicians most often work in concert halls. Musicians also play at wedding receptions, anniversary parties, and other social functions.

Wherever they work, most musicians are self-employed. They use personal web pages, social media, and other digital sources to advertise their skills, book gigs, and connect with other musicians. Some have moved beyond the traditional income sources to build careers through music streaming platforms like Pandora, Amazon, Apple, SoundCloud, and Spotify. These streaming services have websites like Spotify for Artists, specifically created for those who wish to get their music played on the popular digital radio stations.

Those who stream their music often work with distributors who handle technical issues, such as music licensing. The distributors track the number of times a song is streamed and pay a royalty—a small stipend—for each play.

Working Conditions

Many musicians are creatures of the night. They go to work in clubs at around 8 p.m., set up their equipment, and play from 9 p.m. until 1 a.m. Those who play in New Orleans, Las Vegas, and other late-night cities might play until 4 a.m. Then it is time to load up the equipment and go home. In such situations, musicians go to bed when the sun is coming up and might sleep past noon. This can be especially stressful for musicians with families that keep more normal hours.

Earnings

Many musicians dream of making it as superstars who earn tens of millions of dollars per year. But in reality, musicians and singers earned an average wage of $27 an hour in 2017, according to the US Bureau of Labor Statistics (BLS). The BLS notes that many who work in the field only find part-time or intermittent work. Those who work as orchestra musicians or in playhouses might earn up to $100 an hour, depending on where they live.

Opportunities for Advancement

Statistics compiled by the Next Big Sound, which tracks the online activities of a large number of musicians, show that more than 90 percent of musicians who promote themselves on social media remain undiscovered. However, success is relative. Musicians who work hard and have an element of luck can advance in their careers from teaching music and playing in local bars to working as session musicians in recording studios or backing the next Taylor Swift.

What Is the Future Outlook for Musicians?

The BLS says employment of musicians is expected to grow by around 6 percent by 2026. The demand for studio musicians who can record music for commercials, promotional websites, television shows, and movies is expected to grow slightly faster.

American Guild of Music (AGM)
PO Box 599
Warren, MI 48090
website: www.americanguild.org

This organization is open to musicians, music teachers, music publishers, instrument makers, and students. The AGM sponsors music contests, concerts, teacher workshops, and traveling displays of musical instruments and music.

CareersInMusic.com
PO Box 45362
Las Vegas, NV 89116
website: www.careersinmusic.com

This website features articles with career advice, listings of music schools, industry contacts, and numerous occupations that might be pursued by a professional musician.

MajoringInMusic.com
PO Box 2277
Boulder, CO 80306-2277
website: www.majoringinmusic.com

This website caters to those searching for music schools, summer music programs, scholarships, and other information a student needs to make smart decisions about establishing a sustainable musical career.

Youth Music Project
2015 Eighth Ave.
West Linn, OR 97068
website: www.youthmusicproject.org

This Oregon-based organization is dedicated to providing rock, pop, and country music education to young people. The project offers a high school intern program, tuition assistance, instrument use, and a stage for performance opportunities.

Instrument Repair Tech

What Does an Instrument Repair Tech Do?

Anyone watching a big-time rock band play live might notice an individual running out onto the stage between songs with a guitar in hand. This person helps the band's guitarist strap on the fresh guitar before running offstage with the previously used instrument. The new guitar might have a different tone needed for the next song, or it might simply be replacing an out-of-tune instrument. Fans watching the show might assume the person helping the guitarist is a roadie who sets up and tears down stage equipment for a living. But the instrument switcher is a guitar tech who plays an important role in the live music industry. In addition to facilitating guitar exchanges, guitar techs change strings, repair and renovate instruments, and adjust the height of the strings (the action) on a guitar. Most guitar techs also work with electronics and clean, repair, and replace parts, including sound pickups on a guitar, cables, effects pedals, and amplifiers.

Most guitar techs establish strong personal connections with their musician clients. Brian Farmer is a guitar tech for Allman Brothers

At a Glance

Instrument Repair Tech

Minimum Educational Requirements
Broad music education is beneficial

Personal Qualities
Enjoy working alone; manual dexterity performing precise tasks; good interpersonal skills

Working Conditions
Conventional business hours for some; highly irregular hours and long periods of travel for concert techs

Salary
$36,530 in 2017

Number of Jobs
8,240 in 2017

Future Job Outlook
4 percent growth through 2024

Band guitarist Warren Haynes. He explained his job on the Premier Guitar website: "I can watch Warren's face and his hands and know if the guitar is setup perfect or if he's struggling or fighting the guitar—I can sense that in his playing."

Guitar techs like Farmer work long hours. They are at sound checks in the afternoon before a concert. As the equipment is set up, techs test all the guitars, pedals, and amps to make sure everything is working smoothly. When a show begins, guitar techs can be found just offstage or crouching behind a bank of amplifiers. They watch the entire performance attentively while listening to the music through in-ear monitors. After a show is over, techs clean the instruments, carefully pack all the guitars into road cases, and help load the instruments onto a truck. After calling it a night around 3 a.m., techs sleep on a crew bus, wake up in a new city, and start all over again.

Most instrument repair techs lead much more sedate lives, earning their living in small studios and repair shops. In Mankato, Minnesota, Benjamin Williams has been repairing and building custom acoustic guitars and ukuleles in his basement workshop since 2005. As Williams told Mankato's *Free Press* newspaper in 2019, "I liked woodworking and I was in a few bands in the area, so I just thought I'd put two and two together." Williams sells basic guitars for around $1,200, with prices topping out at more than $4,000. These handmade guitars are of a much higher quality than those that are mass produced. They are built to last and have a unique sound due to the wood finishes and construction techniques used by Williams.

Although his instrument-building methods originated in the seventeenth century, Williams uses modern marketing techniques to promote his business. He sells his guitars and ukuleles in twenty-first-century style, posting pictures and sound clips on Facebook and Instagram.

Williams and others who build and repair acoustic stringed instruments are sometimes called luthiers. But this term is not used to describe piano technicians like Emily Hillbert, who tunes, repairs, and restores pianos. Hillbert is one of only four female members in the fourteen-person Vermont chapter of the Piano Technicians Guild. She began her career as a piano teacher in Los Angeles. After several clients asked her to help them fix or buy pianos, she took a course on piano technology. As Hillbert explained to Vermont Public Radio, "I found that it was a profession that I really, really enjoyed because I could work with my hands. I was constantly problem-solving, which kind of gave me the challenge of figuring out things, and I liked the mechanical aspect." In addition to tuning and repairing pianos in clients' homes, Hillbert contracts with the music department at Middlebury College, which has many pianos that need constant attention. She also fixes and tunes pianos for summer camps, churches, and other institutions.

Public schools provide a major source of income for brass repair technician Ronnie Atwood, who works at Tarpley Music in San Angelo, Texas. When regional schools are out for the summer, music teachers send between fifteen hundred and two thousand tubas, saxophones, trombones, French horns, trumpets, and other brass instruments to Atwood for repairs and restoration. To keep up with the demand, Atwood takes on apprentices to wash and polish instruments and fix dents, stuck valves, and bent mouthpieces.

Whereas Atwood works on student instruments, Perry Ritter has been a saxophone specialist to the stars since the 1970s. He replaces and adjusts delicate keys, rods, pins, springs, cork, and leather pads. Ritter learned his mechanical skills by working in his father's machine shop. He played saxophone in his high school band but decided he was not good enough to earn a living playing music. So Ritter decided to attend musical instrument repair school.

Working out of a tiny shop in Brooklyn, New York, Ritter has repaired extremely rare and expensive saxophones for jazz greats such as Pharaoh Sanders and Michael Brecker. Ritter also makes custom instruments; his flame-shooting saxophone, known as the Flame-O-Phone, is used during encores by musician Stefan Zeniuk. Saxophones are in the woodwind family, and Ritter repairs other woodwinds, including clarinets, flutes, oboes, and bassoons.

Whether they are refurbishing an oboe or tuning up a guitar for a rock-and-roll hero, instrument repair techs rely on a host of skills. The website for the National Association of Professional Band Instrument Repair Technicians (NAPBIRT) sums up the job this way: "A repair tech is a problem-solver, mechanic, acoustician, plumber, musician, bodyworker, innovator, painter, jeweler, tool and die maker, electroplater, counselor, buffer, chemist, designer, carpenter, and machine tool operator all in one."

How Do You Become an Instrument Repair Tech?

Education

Instrument repair techs are required to have an intimate understanding of the instruments they work with so they can make minute adjustments that professional players appreciate. This means anyone wishing to fix saxophones—or trumpets, guitars, drums, or any other instrument—needs to be able to play proficiently. Beyond that, there are no formal educational requirements to become an instrument repair tech. Some are self-taught, but others study instrument repair as part of a music education.

Prospective instrument repair techs can visit websites such as the Guild of American Luthiers or NAPBIRT to find sources of online instruction or instrument repair schools. As classical guitar maker Matt Rubendall told CareersinMusic.com, "It is an industry you need to be fairly competent to work in . . . and the schools are important for that."

Some state and community colleges feature two-year programs that offer an associate's degree in band instrument repair. Coursework focuses on the fundamentals of band instrument construction. Students also work in machine shops fabricating instrument parts with lathes, drill presses, grinders, sanders, and other tools. Degree programs also include courses in small business development, marketing, math, and general education.

Guitar techs who work for rock bands often evolve into the position. On the Premier Guitar website, Warren Termini, the guitar tech for Bill Kelliher of the heavy metal band Mastodon, describes his career arc: "I took to helping my high school . . . [musician] friends set up and tear down shows all over Boston. It was more of something to do . . . but after doing that for a bit things took off and I landed more and more gigs that were bigger and bigger. Things tended to snowball when I was involved in that early scene."

Volunteer Work and Internships

Many instrument repair techs begin their careers as apprentices working for little or no money. Brass repair technician Atwood is always looking for students who want to learn the trade. Rubendall, who lives in New York City, adds that most instrument makers love what they do and are eager to help newcomers: "I don't take on apprentices because I don't have the time . . . but you're more than welcome to come to the shop, hang out for a day or two and ask me any question you want."

Skills and Personality

Instrument repair techs often work alone for long periods of time while focusing intently on tasks that require a high degree of precision. As Rubendall explains, "It's an obsessive-compulsive personality in some sense. You have to like working by yourself." On the other hand, instrument repair techs require the social skills to work closely with their clients, listen to their concerns, and connect on a musical level. As Farmer says, "The best thing and number one key to a good relationship between a tech and his guitarist is trust. [Warren Haynes] trusts . . . that all his gear—new or vintage—will be in top form through all the traveling."

On the Job

Employers

Instrument repair technicians are often self-employed. Some work out of small storefronts where they do repairs and receive

An instrument repair tech works on a guitar. Many techs both build and repair instruments, and they often establish strong personal connections with their clients.

customers; others have shops in their homes. Instrument repair technicians might also work for manufacturers like Taylor Guitars in El Cajon, California, or Steinway Musical Instruments, which makes pianos in Waltham, Massachusetts. Concert techs who wish to work with bands and orchestras can find work by contacting a group's tour manager or sound production crew.

Working Conditions

Instrument repair technicians who work out of shops usually keep regular business hours. Some, though, might open later in the day and stay open on nights and weekends to cater to musicians who do not keep regular hours. Professionals in this field can be exposed to power tools and glues, varnishes, and other chemicals that require them to wear protective gear.

Earnings

The average salary for an instrument repair tech depends on the job. But according to the US Bureau of Labor Statistics (BLS), those who repair percussion, stringed, or wind instruments earned a median salary of $36,530 in 2017. Highly experienced repair technicians in the field's highest earnings percentile averaged around $59,300 per year. The BLS figures do not factor in salaries for guitar or drum techs who work with popular performers, but seasoned concert techs can earn up to $100,000 annually.

Opportunities for Advancement

Some concert techs begin their careers as roadies, workers who lug amps and set up stage shows. Others work on the sound crew, adjusting microphone levels and speaker volume. A few concert techs, because they are intimately familiar with the music played by their employers, end up playing in the band. Rock stars like David Gilmour, Noel Gallagher, and Henry Rollins have all moved their concert techs into positions in their backup bands.

What Is the Future Outlook for Instrument Repair Techs?

The BLS predicts 4 percent employment growth for instrument repair techs through 2024, which is slower than average. Demand is expected to remain flat as a growing number of people learn to fix their own instruments by watching online videos.

Find Out More

Chicago School of Violin Making
3636 Oakton St.
Skokie, IL 60076
website: www.csvm.org

The Chicago School of Violin Making offers a three-year course that prepares students to start a career in violin making and repair. The website features information about curriculum, admission, and tuition.

Guild of American Luthiers
8222 S. Park Ave.
Tacoma, WA, 98408
website: www.luth.org

Prospective builders of guitars, mandolins, and other stringed instruments can learn about the luthier trade from this educational organization. The guild promotes the art, craft, and science of stringed instrument construction and offers books, instrument plans, and *American Lutherie* magazine.

National Association of Professional Band
Instrument Repair Technicians (NAPBIRT)
PO Box 51
2026 Eagle Rd.
Normal, IL 61761
website: www.napbirt.org

NAPBIRT is an educational association dedicated to promoting the craft of band instrument repair. The association publishes *TechniCom Magazine* for repair professionals, and its website contains educational opportunities, job listings, technical tips, and information about regional repair clinics.

Piano Technicians Guild
4444 Forest Ave.
Kansas City, KS 66916
website: www.ptg.org

The guild is a leading source of information about piano service and technology. Its website features a database of piano industry businesses and provides educational and career information and links to the periodical *Piano Technicians Journal.*

Artists and Repertoire Director

What Does an Artists and Repertoire Director Do?

Almost everyone who owns a television is familiar with Simon Cowell's work. His singing competition *Idol* shows, which include *American Idol,* are seen all over the world, from Armenia to Vietnam. Cowell also created the *X-Factor* series and *America's Got Talent* and *Britain's Got Talent.* Cowell has appeared as a judge on various versions of *Idol, X-Factor,* and *Got Talent,* and he is widely known for his caustic comments about the singing abilities of the contestants. What most people do not know is that Cowell is considered the world's greatest artists and repertoire (A&R) director by music industry insiders. Acts discovered and developed by Cowell, including One Direction, Kelly Clarkson, and Fifth Harmony, have sold more than 500 million records worldwide.

A&R directors like Cowell help record labels build a profitable repertoire, or catalog, of songs performed by a

At a Glance

Artists and Repertoire Director

Minimum Educational Requirements
Bachelor's degree in music, communications, business, or marketing preferred

Personal Qualities
Musical, math, and business skills; outgoing personality; good communicator; able to take criticism

Working Conditions
An all-encompassing career that requires work on nights, weekends, and holidays in music venues, corporate offices, and music studios

Salary Range
$31,050 to $201,250 in 2018

Number of Jobs
Approximately 15,450 in 2017*

Future Job Outlook
4 percent growth through 2026*

* Includes talent agents and business managers of artists, performers, and athletes

wide range of artists. In this role, A&R directors are responsible for much of the music people hear on a daily basis. But few people understand the role of A&R directors in the $15 billion global music industry. While talented artists, songwriters, and record producers generate great music, the A&R director is the matchmaker behind the scenes who assembles the ideal creative team to produce the biggest hits.

Good A&R directors have a keen ear for music and use this skill to discover recording artists and help them make hit records. In addition to discovering talent, A&R directors connect artists with successful songwriters and help artists select songs to record. When Aaron Bay-Schuck worked in A&R for Atlantic Records, he paired Selena Gomez with German music producer Zedd to write and record "I Want You to Know," which sold over 1 million copies.

A&R directors also connect talent to record producers who oversee the recording process. Music journalist David Mellor explains the importance of choosing the right producer on the website of the *Audio Masterclass Newsletter*: "The producer can potentially make or break the record. . . . If a producer has a history of success with guitar orientated bands, then it would be a safe option to choose him to produce [a] newly signed guitar band. If a producer has had dance floor success, then he could be exactly right for [a] new solo artist."

A&R directors generally work with a number of musical artists who have been selected for their ability to achieve their record company's commercial goals. This means A&R directors have vast powers that allow them to single-handedly shape their record label's future while influencing the way music is created and consumed. And Cowell provides a perfect example, as Warner Music Group's chief executive officer (CEO), Max Lousada, tells the Music Business Worldwide website: "Simon is a pioneer of the idea that talent can come from anywhere, that music can go global from day one. His journey has been all about the joy of discovery, shared in real time with huge audiences of fans. . . . He's a brilliant A&R who understands the ingredients of stardom, the importance of great songs, and the power of image."

Most A&R directors are not as famous as Cowell, but they all share similar skills. They are creative people who are intimately familiar with music, music history, and various genres. A&R directors are also businesspeople who understand what sells. They can listen to dozens of musicians, singers, and songwriters and pick the artists who have the best chance of succeeding. In 2019 Margaret Tomlin was the twenty-six-year-old A&R director at Sony Music Nashville. Tomlin told California's *Coronado Eagle & Journal* newspaper how she hunts talent:

> We look at Spotify for new artists we need to be aware of and we are looking at Instagram and Facebook for how many followers an artist has. . . . And we need to be aware online and reacting to clubs and shows held in smaller venues around the country. There is no one formula to sign an artist. But either the artist with a guitar or an artist with their piano needs to blow us away.

A&R directors are good with numbers. After they sign someone, they create a budget for all of the expenses associated with developing the artist's career. Budgets pay for studio time, session musicians, producers, mixing a record, marketing, promotion, and even costumes, hairstyling, and makeup. A&R directors also need to be good managers. They often oversee large A&R departments with numerous employees, including talent scouts, A&R assistants, and A&R administrators who handle financial and clerical tasks.

How Do You Become an A&R Director?

Education

There are no formal educational requirements to become an A&R director. However, the world of A&R is extremely difficult to break into, and those who overcome the competition generally have impressive math, business, and musical skills. A&R director Andrew Corria offers this advice on CareersInMusic.com: "Go to school and be educated. A lot of record labels like to have graduates with Communications, Business, and Marketing degrees. They kind of help you to get your foot in the door." Corria also advises students to seek out schools that offer a master of business administration degree that can provide a good foundation for a career as an A&R director.

Many A&R directors are musicians. When Tomlin was a high school student in Washington, DC, she took classical voice training and attended the Young Singers Program at the Washington National Opera. However, she did not want to spend her life auditioning for short-term jobs on the opera stage. This led her to focus on the business side of the music industry.

In 2011 Tomlin attended Syracuse University, where she entered the Martin Bandier Program. This program is named after the CEO of Sony/ATV Music Publishing, who graduated from the school during the 1960s and who was involved in creating the course curriculum. Tomlin describes the Bandier Program: "[It] is a combination of music and business. It includes classes in communication law, the history of music, and entrepreneurship. Only 25 kids per year are brought into the program, so there are never more than 100 students."

Volunteer Work and Internships

The Bandier Program requires students to serve three internships to meet the graduation requirements. Internships are offered by major entertainment companies, such as Warner Music Group and Atlantic Records, and independent labels and music publishers. Tomlin worked for four months in London as an intern at Sony/ATV, where she says "the focus is on writers, finding songs, building a catalog, then pitching the songs to recording artists and getting placement."

Skills and Personality

An A&R director needs to be an outgoing person who can easily work with a wide range of personality types and communicate effectively under stressful conditions. A&R directors have to smooth the ruffled feathers of artists, who can be impulsive, demanding, depressed, or insecure. They often meet with producers, managers, and recording engineers who have competing agendas. A&R directors often field calls from record label executives who expect hits but are concerned about spending and missed deadlines. And they have to do it all behind the scene without expecting much appreciation or public acclaim. As Corria says,

> You have to have really good communications skills and a thick skin because sometimes you're getting it from all angles; you're hearing things from the label, you're hearing things from your boss and you kind of have to smooth things out. . . . You're the person who put these people together, but you're not going to get the press, so you have to be cool being behind-the-scenes.

On the Job

Employers

Some A&R directors are self-employed. They own small record labels or manage acts hoping to make it big. Those who build up an impressive track record and discover new artists with great potential can get hired by major record labels and music publishers. Most of these businesses are located in music centers like Nashville, Los Angeles, New York City, and London. Smaller record labels that focus on local scenes can be found in Seattle, Minneapolis, Memphis, and elsewhere.

Working Conditions

Those who work as A&R directors will say that it is not a nine-to-five job but a full-time, all-encompassing career. As record company executives, A&R directors work around the clock, bouncing between music venues and meeting rooms. As Tomlin explains, "We go to shows [at night] regularly during the week to see the artists in town. And we take a lot of meetings during the day with publishers, managers, attorneys and booking agents." A&R directors visit recording studios to oversee record song production. They work one on one with songwriters who are under pressure to write smash hits. And they often juggle more than a dozen acts, speaking to the press on their behalf, working on deadlines, and taking part in conference calls. According to Corria, "For someone who likes to get their eight or nine hours of sleep, it's not for that person. It can be hectic sometimes for sure. . . . You're always on. You have to go to the label when there are marketing people [visiting]. You have to meet another artist somewhere where they're having a session. You're all over the place."

Earnings

The amount A&R directors earn depends on where they are employed. Those who are self-employed or work for small record labels earn significantly less than those who are employed by major entertainment companies. But exact salary figures are not available. The US Bureau of Labor Statistics (BLS) does not provide salary or other data specific to A&R directors. The most recent figures are from a study of music industry pay scales commissioned by the Berklee College of Music in 2010. Since average wages in all jobs increased by approximately 15 percent between 2010 and 2018, the wages have been adjusted to reflect that increase; therefore, it is estimated that in 2018 an A&R director earned anywhere from $31,050 to $201,250 annually.

Opportunities for Advancement

Many A&R directors begin their careers as entry-level A&R administrators who earn little more than minimum wage. These workers perform menial tasks like booking studio time, analyzing record sales data, coordinating artist travel schedules, and preparing bills and purchase orders. Those who wish to advance their careers can do some after-work talent scouting and bring promising musical acts to their boss's attention. This can result in a promotion to A&R director. And a handful of A&R directors go on to earn large sums of money working with top-selling acts.

What Is the Future Outlook for A&R Directors?

The BLS includes A&R directors in a category that is defined as talent agents and business managers of artists, performers, and athletes. This field is expected to grow by 4 percent through 2026.

Find Out More

Atlantic Records Internship Program
website: www.atlanticrecords.com/internships

Atlantic Records is one of Warner Music Group's most prominent and successful labels. Atlantic's internship program is open to students currently enrolled in an accredited undergraduate or graduate program who wish to learn about the music industry while receiving class credits.

CareersInMusic.com
PO Box 45362
Las Vegas, NV 89116
website: www.careersinmusic.com

This website features articles with career advice, listings of music schools, industry contacts, and numerous occupations that might be pursued by a person wishing to work as an A&R director in the music business.

Kings of A&R (KOAR)
website: http://kingsofar.com

A&R analysts who write for KOAR scour the Internet for emerging artists. The website features hundreds of profiles about everyone from the Killers to Lady Gaga, written from an A&R standpoint.

National Association of Record Industry Professionals (NARIP)
PO Box 2446
Los Angeles, CA 91610
website: www.narip.com

The National Association of Record Industry Professionals promotes education and career advancement in the record industry and related music fields. NARIP offers seminars and workshops, A&R pitch sessions, and job listings.

Music Publicist

What Does a Music Publicist Do?

Almost every modern music fan has heard of sensations like Drake, Halsey, and Cardi B. And there is a reason for that. Like many big stars, these celebrities employ music publicists to keep their names front and center in all types of media. The first job of a music publicist is to create publicity, which the dictionary defines as "an act or device designed to attract public interest." Music publicists create publicity by providing exclusive news—and select gossip—about their clients to radio disc jockeys (DJs), producers at television entertainment shows, and popular YouTubers. Music publicists get their client's music placed in television shows and movies. And they use Instagram, Facebook, Tumblr, and Twitter accounts in their client's name to post tweets, photos, and comments. In a 2019 interview with the Loud Hailer website, music publicist Fiona Bloom described her work for clients like Wayna and Chuck D: "I do everything from the branding opportunities to looking for sponsorships or endorsements. I help them with

At a Glance

Music Publicist

Minimum Educational Requirements
Bachelor's degree in communications, public relations, or related field preferred

Personal Qualities
Hard worker; self-starter; avid reader; good communicator; creative; musically inclined

Working Conditions
Travel and long hours working nights, weekends, and holidays in offices and at concert venues and parties

Salary
$59,300 median annual income in 2016*

Number of Jobs
259,600 in 2016*

Future Job Outlook
9 percent job growth through 2026*

* Includes all public relations specialists

touring. . . . I also do their global stuff, I look out for opportunities internationally, opening up markets in South America or South Africa or Asia."

If you are searching for more insight into the music publicity business, you only need to click on the *Rolling Stone* magazine website. You might see articles with titles like "Best New Artist You Need to Know" or "Hottest Single of the Year." "That is all 100% work of a publicist," says Ariel Hyatt of the artist development company Cyber PR. "The editor did not go [out and] walk around to find the best anything. The publicist worked very, very hard with the editor to place [their client in the article]."

Hyatt says an important part of her job is keeping her ear to the ground. This means she follows the latest trends and listens for clues to what the next big thing will be. By knowing what the media likes—and what the public will buy—Hyatt can help her clients hone their images. She can even offer advice about creating new music and videos that will appeal to the widest audience.

Music publicists need to develop a wide range of contacts. Bloom says she knows over three thousand people in the entertainment business. Her address book includes names of magazine editors, bloggers, radio and television personalities, marketing directors, brand ambassadors, festival promoters, awards show producers, and musicians. As Bloom explains, "I know it sounds crazy to say that I have . . . 3,000 real solid relationships of people that I've either had lunch with, people that I've traveled with, people that I've had extended conversations with. . . . But honestly, I would not have been able to achieve most of what I'm doing today if I did not have those 3,000 relationships."

How Do You Become a Music Publicist?

Education

Like many others who work in the music industry, music publicists are often musicians themselves. Bloom learned to sing and play violin and piano when she was in elementary school. And,

A music publicist works the phone to create buzz for her clients. Music publicists spend a lot of time on the phone and meeting in person with entertainment industry professionals who can bring notice to the musicians they represent.

like many others, she came to realize she was not good enough to earn a living playing music. As Bloom puts it, "I thought . . . if I can't be a musician let me be in the music business. If . . . I can't be on stage, let me be behind the stage." This led Bloom to major in speech communication in college while earning a minor in broadcast journalism.

Bloom's college degree was helpful, but she worked at numerous jobs in the music industry that helped pave her road to success as a music publicist. While everyone's career path is different, Bloom illustrates the type of hard work, experience, creativity, and vision needed to become a successful music publicist.

While still in school, Bloom hosted a popular music program on her college radio station. After graduation she was hired as an assistant music director by a commercial radio station in Atlanta, Georgia. At this job, Bloom worked as a DJ and created playlists for other DJs. She also spent her days dealing with music publicists who worked to get their client's records played on the air. Using the connections she made at the radio station, Bloom ran a side gig as a party promoter, persuading people to attend shows by bands and DJs. She was paid a small stipend for every guest who came to the club. She also got a gig on a public radio station creating and hosting *World Party*, a daily show featuring international music that became very popular. Using her ever-widening group of industry contacts, Bloom cofounded a music public relations (PR) firm at the age of twenty-five. She helped launch the careers of clients such as Drivin' and Cryin' and Michelle Malone. And she continued to work as a DJ and party promoter, which helped her music publicist career: "[I] became the influencer in the Atlanta market. So I'd be breaking stuff on the radio all day long and then labels would come to me and put me on lists for . . . premieres for things or invites to certain private events and then artists would come on my show and I'd interview them all day long and then years later they'd become world-renowned artists." Eventually, Bloom was noticed by an executive from the New York office of EMI, where she was hired as a manager of marketing. This led to a gig at a start-up label, Zero Hour Records, where Bloom built the music publicity department from the ground up. She opened her own agency, the Bloom Effect, in 2007.

Volunteer Work and Internships

Internships offer prospective music publicists valuable hands-on experience in music marketing, streaming, publicity, touring, and artists and repertoire management. Hyatt writes on the Cyber PR website that interns are needed in every facet of the music industry, including PR firms like hers. She notes that almost all her colleagues started out as unpaid interns who were able to leverage their positions into paying jobs. Little wonder that Hyatt says she receives "a stupid amount of resumes" whenever she puts out a call for interns, even though "99.9% of all music business internships are unpaid." On the upside, college students who intern at larger companies get college credit for their efforts.

Skills and Personality

Music publicists are tireless self-starters and good communicators who are skilled in the art of persuasion. They rely on phone calls, e-mails, and face-to-face meetings to persuade journalists, booking agents, radio DJs, and others to promote the music made by the artists they represent. Bloom describes the skills she possessed at the beginning of her career: "Relentless hard work, being in your face. . . . I was an arm-twister . . . aggressive but not overly aggressive, annoying but not bad annoying. But yes, in your face all the time because you had to be, otherwise you weren't going to get anywhere. It takes a certain breed of person to be able to do that. A lot of people can't."

Music publicists also need to be avid readers. They have to read newspapers, fashion and entertainment publications, websites, and social media sites to remain cognizant of the latest social, fashion, and musical trends.

On the Job

Employers

Music publicists often work for large entertainment companies like Sony, Warner, and Universal. These firms have a number of departments that handle music publicity, including promotions, marketing, licensing, and sales. Other employers of music publicists include independent record labels, PR firms, artist management companies, booking agencies, radio promotions companies, live music venues, concert promoters, music publishing companies, music websites, and production companies. Hyatt offers this advice for anyone seeking a job as a music publicist: "If you love a specific band or artist, look up who they work with and put those companies on your list because nothing is more thrilling and satisfying than working for your FAVORITE artists and bands (I still get a thrill out of that and I've been working in the music industry for 21 years)."

Working Conditions

As Bloom's experience illustrates, music publicists do not put in forty-hour workweeks. Most live and breathe music publicity from morning meetings at the office until the last encore is played at the nightclub. Music publicists work days, nights, weekends, and holidays to attend concerts, music industry parties, and promotional events. Those who represent major recording artists tour extensively and might be away from home many months out of the year.

Earnings

The US Bureau of Labor Statistics (BLS) classifies music publicists as PR specialists and says their median annual salary was $59,300 in 2017. However, this figure also includes people who do PR work for the government, advertising agencies, and professional organizations. Although the BLS does not offer official numbers, publicists who work in the music industry can earn much higher pay than the average for all PR specialists.

Music publicists who own their own firms or who freelance for record labels offer a menu of services and charge a different rate for each project. For example, a well-known publicist hired for a full-time, three-month campaign to promote a band's upcoming album release or national tour can charge between $2,000 and $3,500 per month. A music publicist who places a big story about a band in a national publication might charge a one-time fee of $500. For music publicists who have five to ten clients, these charges can add up to a six-figure annual salary.

Opportunities for Advancement

Most music publicists learn the ropes working at entry-level jobs for large entertainment companies. They might be assistants, receptionists, or administrators who are given the opportunity to take over publicity for a recently signed act. Eventually, the publicist will be given more responsibilities, possibly managing teams of people or working with a client at the national level. The most successful music publicists start their own firms and earn top dollar working with major celebrities.

What Is the Future Outlook for Music Publicists?

The BLS predicts that the number of jobs for all PR specialists will grow by 9 percent through 2026. Although the bureau does not provide specific growth forecasts for music publicists, the need for musicians to create and maintain a strong presence in social media and other outlets is only expected to grow in the coming years. This will create a steady demand for specialists in music publicity.

Find Out More

Alliance for Women in Media
2365 Harrodsburg Rd.
Lexington, KY 40504
website: https://allwomeninmedia.org

This nonprofit organization is dedicated to the support and career advancement for women in all areas of the media, including PR. The Alliance for Women in Media Foundation offers educational programs and scholarships to students planning careers in the media and related fields.

Cyber PR
389 Twelfth St.
Brooklyn, NY 11215
website: https://cyberprmusic.com

Cyber PR is an artist development firm run by music publicist Ariel Hyatt. The website offers Cyber PR Labs, which are a series of master classes in which students learn from top industry experts. Additionally, Hyatt's numerous educational blogs offer excellent insight into the music PR business.

PR Council
135 W. Forty-First St.
New York, NY 10036
website: http://prcouncil.net

The PR Council consists of more than one hundred of the nation's leading communications firms. Its website features blogs, webinars, and job listings. Its Student Innovation Challenge awards prizes to students who create an exceptional video and PR campaign on a given topic.

Public Relations Society of America (PRSA)
120 Wall St., 21st Floor
New York, NY 10005
website: www.prsa.org

The PRSA is a professional organization that caters to the communications community. The society's website provides comprehensive information about the PR business, and the PRSA Foundation offers access to scholarships and grants for college students pursuing a career in PR.

Artistic Director

What Does an Artistic Director Do?

Every year the Children's Theater in Minneapolis performs "The 500 Hats of Bartholomew Cubbins," a play based on the beloved Dr. Seuss book. The lead character, Bartholomew Cubbins, is required to remove his hat in the presence of the king. But each time Bartholomew doffs his hat, another one magically appears. Peter C. Brosius has been the artistic director of the Children's Theater since 1997. Like Bartholomew Cubbins, Brosius wears many hats, which is to say he does many different jobs.

Depending on the day—or the time of day—an artistic director like Brosius might perform the tasks of a producer, a casting director, a costume designer, a script editor, a fund-raiser, an actor, a choreographer, a teacher, or an accountant. When artistic directors wear their producer's hat, they pick four to six plays for the next performance season. Artistic directors also supervise the development of original works. For example, "The 500 Hats of Bartholomew Cubbins" was first staged in 1979 by Brosius's predecessor, who commissioned the writers, composers, and choreographers who created the play.

At a Glance

Artistic Director

Minimum Educational Requirements
Bachelor of fine arts degree preferred

Personal Qualities
Creative vision; eye for talent; leadership qualities; good communicator; strong business and management skills

Working Conditions
Long hours in theaters and offices attending meetings and overseeing performances; travel is often required

Salary
$58,860 in 2017*

Number of Jobs
134,700 in 2016*

Future Job Outlook
12 percent growth through 2026*

* Includes producers and directors employed in performing arts and related industries

After finalizing a theater company's season, artistic directors put on the casting director's hat. In this important role they audition and hire the actors, dancers, conductors, and orchestra musicians who will bring a play to life. In 2015 Brosius explained to the *Pioneer Press* newspaper in St. Paul, Minnesota, why he spent months auditioning actors for Bartholomew Cubbins: "Part of what we want to do is deliver physical humor but also tell a beautiful, poetic, surprising and touching story. . . . I needed people who could break your heart and also tickle your funny bone."

In addition to their creative duties, artistic directors need to focus on economics. Most performing arts organizations, whether they are dance companies, theater companies, opera companies, or symphony orchestras, are nonprofits. This means they depend on monetary grants from state and local government arts councils and the National Endowment for the Arts (NEA), a federal arts agency. Nonprofit performing arts organizations also rely on donations from individuals, corporations, and charitable trusts like the MacArthur Foundation. Artistic directors must be familiar with all grant providers and oversee efforts to obtain money from these individuals and organizations.

Artistic directors are the public face of their performing arts companies at fund-raisers, benefits, board meetings, press conferences, and in radio and television interviews. They are in charge of administration, supervising grant writers, accountants, lawyers, and others who deal with money and paperwork. Artistic directors are also educators. Most arts organizations run educational outreach programs that bring performances to schools, provide classes for students, and put on productions featuring young people. Artistic directors are responsible for creating, scheduling, and supervising such programs.

How Do You Become an Artistic Director?

Education
Most artistic directors fall in love with the theater when they are young. They attend plays, operas, ballets, and the symphony

orchestra. Those who wish to pursue their passion for the arts can learn to act, dance, sing, or play an instrument. Students can also participate in theatrical youth programs and perform with children's theaters that are found in most medium and large cities. One example, the SteppingStone Theater in St. Paul, offers semester-long classes and summer performance programs. SteppingStone presents two hundred performances a year, all featuring students ages eight through eighteen. As Stepping-Stone artistic director Richard Hitchler told *Backstage* magazine, "SteppingStone has always been more than simply a theatre experience for children, it's a safe haven for developing young minds, and a building block for tomorrow's great leaders."

Theater-loving students who attend college can pursue a bachelor of fine arts (BFA) degree. The Berklee College of Music in Boston provides good examples of degree programs that can benefit prospective artistic directors. Berklee offers a BFA in contemporary theater that emphasizes four main activities: training, performing, creating, and producing. The aspects that focus on creating and producing are particularly helpful to those who dream of becoming artistic directors. These courses teach theatrical storytelling, scripting, staging, set design, directing, community engagement, arts management, and finance. Berklee also offers a master of fine arts in musical theater. This five-semester program features advanced training in performance, theater fundamentals, and entertainment industry practices.

Volunteer Work and Internships

On-the-job experience is important to anyone wishing to work as an artistic director, and almost every community arts organization is open to volunteers and interns. Websites for organizations such as Americans for the Arts and the NEA list numerous internship and volunteer opportunities offered throughout the nation. Individual performing arts companies also encourage volunteers and interns. For example, the American Repertory Theater in Cambridge, Massachusetts, offers a variety of summer, fall, and spring internship positions to high school students and undergraduate and graduate students. Interns work in various departments, including artistic management, education and community programs, marketing and public relations, and sound technology.

There are exciting opportunities for students who wish to travel while they learn. The Performing Arts Abroad program provides diverse internship opportunities to students who can pay their own way. These include a music development internship in South Africa; a performing arts internship in Florence, Italy; and a theater internship in Barcelona, Spain. Dance student Bethany Green took her internship at a dance school in Barcelona. She described her experience on the Performing Arts Abroad website: "I danced with new friends, learned exciting new styles of dance, and improved my Spanish language abilities. . . . I was also able to spend time in the office of the dance school, answering phones and interacting with [students]. . . . I am eager to put the confidence and skills I gained in Barcelona to use in my life here in the United States."

Skills and Personality

Artistic directors are multitaskers who combine the talents of an inspired visionary with management and business skills. On the creative side, artistic directors are required to put on shows that dazzle the public with stellar performances, staging, and set design. Artistic directors often participate directly in the creative process, providing advice and direction to actors, dancers, singers, and backstage staff. This requires strong written and verbal communication skills and leadership qualities. These talents are also necessary for managing an arts organization, answering to the company's board of directors, and articulating a unique vision for the company's future.

In addition to their many other skills, artistic directors are often gifted educators. Artistic director Michael Unger at the York Theater in New York City launched the Musical Theatre Training Program. This program provides year-round youth classes as well as a children's theater program that performs for children in local schools. Unger explains on the York Theater Company

58

website why he worked to expand theater education opportunities: "I know how formative seeing theater was for me as a young child; and I see it time and time again in the work that I do in other theaters with thousands of eager young faces coming to see shows for the first time."

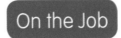

Employers

Artistic directors oversee performing arts organizations that include symphony orchestras, opera companies, dance companies, and theater companies. Many are promoted to artistic director from within the organization after working at lesser positions for many years. Others are hired by a company's board of directors after working as freelancers who have built a reputation as successful independent artistic directors.

Some performers start their own artistic companies, where they may serve as artistic director. Cleo Parker Robinson is a professional dancer and choreographer who founded the award-winning Cleo Robinson Dance Ensemble in Denver in 1970. Still going strong as artistic director in 2019, Robinson guides her company's professional dance ensemble, a youth ensemble, a school of dance, an international summer dance institute, and a variety of youth outreach programs. Robinson described her inspiration in an interview with Ohio's *Dayton Business Journal* in 2019: "I was always interested in not only creating a dance company, but a village, a place where people could create and come together. . . . We wanted to be the heartbeat of the community."

Working Conditions

The work life of artistic directors is dictated by the size of their organizations, but few put in just a forty-hour workweek. Artistic directors work long hours as a company's chief executive officer, administrator, conductor, director, choreographer, and more. There is a great deal of pressure associated with selecting, producing, and staging successful performances. As the old saying goes, the show must go on, even when performers, stage hands, donors, audience members, and others create problems.

Artistic directors at large organizations have it a little easier. They can employ assistants to supervise personnel and take care of administrative tasks. These directors have a degree of fame and spend time traveling, building relationships with donors, and negotiating new artistic projects. They also attend workshops, conventions, and industry events such as the Tony Awards.

Earnings

The US Bureau of Labor Statistics (BLS) does not provide salary information specifically for artistic directors who work for performing arts companies. The BLS does have a category for producers and directors employed in the performing arts, spectator sports, and related industries. Those who work in this general job category earned an average annual salary of $58,860 in 2017. Producers and directors in the top 10 percent earned more than $164,290. Those in the bottom 10 percent earned less than $33,730.

Opportunities for Advancement

Artistic directors often begin their careers as actors, singers, musicians, or dancers. Some work as administrators or fundraisers for theater or dance companies. Unger began his career as a freelance theater and opera director. After gaining national attention as a director and producer of Broadway musicals, Unger was hired as the associate artistic director of the York Theater. In this position, Unger supported the work of the artistic director. This helped him land a gig as artistic director on a York Theater concert celebrating one hundred Broadway musicals.

What Is the Future Outlook for Artistic Directors?

The BLS says the job outlook for all producers and directors is expected to grow by 12 percent through 2026. However, the bureau notes that most of this growth is expected in the motion picture and television industry. The BLS says that job growth is expected to be slower for artistic directors who work in small- and medium-sized theaters because these companies are expected to have an increasingly difficult time selling tickets and finding funding in the future. The picture for large theaters in big cities like New York, Chicago, and Los Angeles is brighter because these institutions have more stable sources of funding.

Find Out More

Americans for the Arts
1000 Vermont Ave. NW
Washington, DC 20005
website: www.americansforthearts.org

Americans for the Arts is an advocacy organization that works to build stronger communities through access to the arts and art education. Its website hosts the Art Services Directory, which links to community arts organizations throughout the country. Prospective art directors can find a job bank, internship information, and resources for grants and scholarships.

Association of Performing Arts Professionals (APAP)
919 Eighteenth St. NW
Washington, DC 20006
website: www.apap365.org

APAP is devoted to developing and promoting a strong performing arts industry. The association offers a webinar archive, a jobs bank, professional development resources, and the Creative Campus program to support innovative performance-based projects on US campuses.

National Endowment for the Arts (NEA)
400 Seventh St. SW
Washington, DC 20506
website: www.arts.gov

The NEA is an independent agency of the US government that offers support for the arts and funding for art projects. Students interested in folk and traditional arts, media arts, music, theater, and other artistic fields can find information on the NEA website. The agency also provides information about regional and state art agencies, artist communities, and arts education.

Theater Communications Group (TCG)
520 Eighth Ave.
New York, NY 10018
website: www.tcg.org

The TCG promotes the interests of over seven hundred non-profit theaters nationwide. The group publishes *American Theater* magazine, the theatrical employment bulletin *ARTSEARCH,* and the annual *Special Report on Education.* Its website features information on grants, research, and advocacy.

Video Game Sound Designer

What Does a Video Game Sound Designer Do?

If you love video games, you have probably played *Assassin's Creed*, the action adventure franchise that has sold more than 120 million copies since its debut in 2007. While millions have thrilled to the video and sound effects of *Assassin's Creed*, few have ever heard of Elitsa Alexandrova. But the Bulgarian-born Alexandrova is a one-woman audio department who created all the sounds and composed the background music for *Assassin's Creed: Rogue* and *Assassin's Creed Origins: The Curse of the Pharaohs*. Alexandrova is a video game sound designer. Like others who work in her profession, she uses her creative talents and technical skills to produce compelling background music, sound effects, and voice-overs for video games.

The job of a video game sound designer is somewhat similar to that of a film and television sound designer. However, sound designers for television and movies create soundtracks while watching the completed shows. That means they can sit in a recording studio and watch a car chase, a party, or a gun battle on a monitor. Using visual clues, they can create music and sounds that enhance the emotional impact of each scene. Video game sound designers do not have this luxury. They have to create noises for several hundred characters and items that emit sound without seeing the game unfolding before them. On the StackExchange game developer website, sound designer Jay Jennings calls his job creating sounds "in isolation": "This . . . approach seems to exercise a different part of the creative brain process. It forces you to . . . create in the near-abstract. It's quite a different thing to create sound design from a . . . full-motion film reel."

Video game sound designers are involved with game development from the very beginning. Before any recording takes place, they attend numerous concept meetings with game designers, producers, and creative directors. They take notes and offer suggestions while learning the crucial qualities of the game under consideration. After a video game is approved for production, sound designers are given a general story line or a detailed script created by game writers. They also work from drawings, gifs, video clips, and other artistic elements. The sound designer uses this information to break the game down into a number of sections, including locations, environments, characters, creatures, weapons, and vehicles. Each one of these elements needs unique music, voices, ambient sounds, and sound effects.

Sound designers create soundtracks in recording studios on machines called digital audio workstations (DAWs), which record, edit, and mix sounds. These systems consist of computerized mixing consoles that run sound production software like Acid Pro or Ableton Live. When sound designers begin work on a game, they first sort through online libraries of sound effects that may be used for free or purchased for commercial use. For example, the BBC Sound Effects library offers more than sixteen thousand sounds, including rowdy crowds, farm animals, sounds of birds and insects in meadows, and all manner of machinery. These sounds can be used singly or mixed together into the thumps, bumps, whaps, crashes, crackles, booms, and swooshes needed for a project.

If the perfect sound is not available from a catalog, video game sound designers create unique noises live in the studio. Sound designer Jason Graves worked on the high-profile game *Far Cry Primal,* which features ritualistic drums and sound effects that include rustling bushes, cracking bones, and shattering clay pots. Graves described his noisemaking tools on the MusicTech.net website: "I'm definitely a fan of drums, percussion and guitars. I've got a collection of electric and acoustic guitars, plus a literal desktop full of guitar [effects] pedals, amps and [speaker] cabinets." In addition to using the effects pedals with guitars, Graves runs drum sounds and other percussion through distortion boxes, wah-wah pedals, and other effects to create unique sounds. He also uses old-school analog synthesizers made by Moog and Arturia, which produce warmer, vintage sounds when compared to modern digital synthesizers.

Sometimes video game sound designers hire voice actors to record character vocal tracks. If sound designers are working on games that feature weaponry or vehicles, they might go out in the field to capture real-life sounds at gun ranges, race tracks, or even military training sites (after obtaining permission from the US Department of Defense).

Whatever type of soundtrack is being created, sound designers need to have a keen ear. As a sound designer known as Amar explains on StackExchange, "In game audio, you . . . have to consider making sounds rewarding for your players. Some sounds are heard often and can't be annoying, some sounds are heard seldom. [With] some sounds you might want the player to feel excited or joyous, and in others you want them to rip their hair out."

How Do You Become a Video Game Sound Designer?

Education

Video game sound designers are lovers of both music and gaming. They often learn to play music at a young age, as Graves explains: "[I] started obsessing over playing instruments in middle school—piano, drums, handbells and a little Casio keyboard. . . . That Casio was really the beginning. So many sounds and drum beats!" Graves took private drum and piano lessons and played in his high school band.

Video game sound designers often enter the industry as programmers. Many learn common computer programming languages like C++, C#, and Java in high school. Others learn to write code online from websites like Codecademy and Free Code Camp. These sites offer free interactive online learning platforms, community forums, and chat rooms. There are also numerous YouTube videos that teach coding and video game sound design.

Learning coding and how to record and play music in high school is good preparation for college. Most sound designers have a bachelor's degree in music, audio engineering, or related fields. The Berklee College of Music in Boston provides good examples of degree programs that can benefit prospective video game sound designers. The bachelor of music in electronic production and design focuses on the creative use of technology in music production. Students work in classrooms, workshops, studios, and performance spaces to learn electronic music composition, synthesizer programming, and sound design techniques for game audio design and other types of media. Berklee also offers a bachelor of music composition for film, television, and games. The courses in this degree program focus on music theory and the use of DAWs to record, sequence, and mix music for animation and video. By the time students graduate, they have a portfolio of diverse compositions. And employers make hiring decisions based on the quality of the work in a sound designer's portfolio.

Certification and Licensing

Video game sound designers do not need to be certified, but numerous organizations offer professional certification, which can lead to greater employment opportunities and higher salaries. Avid Education awards several audio certifications for users of the ProTools audio editing software, including certified operation and certified expert designations.

Volunteer Work and Internships

Video game sound designer Jaclyn Shumate credits her internship at a video game startup for helping her transition from the college classroom to a real-world job. Shumate told the Game Industry Career Guide website that she was able to learn a great deal about the inner workings of the industry by sitting in on game development meetings. She also worked on projects that she was able to include in her portfolio. Interns like Shumate also make professional connections that help them find full-time employment after they graduate. As Shumate says about her internship, "I've been happily employed in many different roles in game audio ever since."

Skills and Personality

Video game sound designers are called upon to produce inspiring orchestration, subtle sound effects, and heart-stopping explosions. This requires them to have musical talent, an innovative spirit, and a discerning ear. Sound designers spend long hours working independently, wearing headphones, and shutting out the world. While they must be comfortable working in isolation, video game sound designers also work with large teams that include character and game designers, animators, programmers, managers, and more. This means sound designers must be communicative and collaborative when working in group situations. And, of course, they live and breathe video games.

On the Job

Employers

Video game sound designers work as in-house employees or as freelancers who are hired on a project-by-project basis. Although most want to work for large gaming companies, the competition is fierce. Some get a foot in the door by taking an entry-level job as a programmer or assistant. Those who wish to gain enough experience to work for a big company might begin their careers at a start-up game design company. These enterprises usually have smaller budgets and fewer support personnel, but sound designers usually earn more praise for their work than they would at a large company. Sound designers might also find work outside the gaming industry, working for software design firms to integrate sound files and create musical cues for various program functions.

Working Conditions

Those who create soundtracks for video games work full-time in offices and recording studios with occasional fieldwork recording sounds at gun ranges or others sites. Some work from home studios; others work in studios owned by large game companies. Hours can vary, as sound designer Raison Varner explains on CareersInMusic.com: "In a low cycle I'll have fairly normal 8 hour days at a relaxed pace. In a peak cycle, I'll have 8 hour high-intensity days for a while and then 9-12 hour high-intensity days for a week or two preceding a major milestone. Depending on the milestone, I'll sometimes work a couple of Saturdays or a weekend or two in a row."

Earnings

Video game sound designers are senior-level employees with at least three years of experience in audio programming. The US Bureau of Labor Statistics (BLS) does not provide salary information for video game sound designers. However, the BLS says the median salary for those classified as sound engineering technicians was $55,810 in 2017. As with most jobs, salaries vary according to a worker's level of education and experience and the size and location of the employer.

Opportunities for Advancement

Video game sound designers might begin their careers as free-lancers who work on television commercials or as assistants at large gaming companies. Experienced video game sound designers can advance to the position of audio director. These professionals set project goals and deadlines, manage workflow, and oversee a company's audio design teams.

Some video game sound designers who compose long musical pieces attract a fan base that allows them to perform concerts and sell their music. Winifred Phillips, whose work can be heard on *Assassin's Creed, Total War, LittleBigPlanet*, and *The Sims* has released fifteen albums that contain her video game compositions. Other sound designers are members of the Assassin's Creed Symphony. This multimedia symphonic project features an eighty-piece orchestra and choir playing musical scores composed by Alexandrova and others.

What Is the Future Outlook for Video Game Sound Designers?

The BLS says employment for all video game designers is expected to grow by more than 9 percent through 2027.

Find Out More

Codecademy
49 W. Twenty-Seventh St.
New York, NY 10001
website: www.codecademy.com

This online school offers free coding lessons in numerous programming languages, including Git, AngularJS, JavaScript, and CSS. Students can sign up and begin coding within minutes.

Designing Sound
website: http://designingsound.org

Visitors to the Designing Sound website can find news, interviews, reviews, and other resources concerning the art and technique of sound design. Tutorials cover many aspects of digital sound creation and are helpful to anyone pursuing a career as a video game sound designer.

Gamasutra
website: www.gamasutra.com

Gamasutra is a website devoted to all aspects of video game development. The site features daily news, reviews, blogs, a career guide, and a jobs/résumé section. Prospective video game sound designers can find a wealth of educational videos, podcasts, newsletters, articles, and interviews that explore all aspects of the game production industry.

Game Audio Network Guild (GANG)
website: www.audiogang.org

GANG represents sound designers and others who work in the game audio industry. Its website provides access to blogs, a newsletter, networking opportunities, awards, and educational resources to industry professionals and students alike.

Interview with a Songwriter

Gretchen Peters is a Grammy-nominated songwriter. Since she got her first music publishing deal in 1987, Peters has written hit songs for Martina McBride, Bryan Adams, Faith Hill, George Strait, Bonnie Raitt, Trisha Yearwood, Don Henley, Patty Loveless, and the Neville Brothers. Peters leads songwriter workshops and is a member of the Nashville Songwriters Hall of Fame. Peters discussed her career with the author by e-mail. The interview has been edited for length and clarity.

Q: Why did you decide to become a songwriter?
A: I've been writing songs since I was a kid but I wanted to be a singer-songwriter. I really wasn't aware that there was a job called "songwriter." To me, the songwriting was just a part of what artists like Bob Dylan and Joni Mitchell did.

Q: Did you study music in school?
A: During my brief career in college I was a music major (vocal performance) for a year or so. But I was already playing in the bars at night and that siren song was too loud for me to ignore, so I dropped out of school.

Q: Can you describe your typical workday (or night) when you are writing songs?
A: I will generally write in the morning from around ten or eleven until two or three in the afternoon. If things are flowing, I'll go with the flow. I can only spend around four to five hours writing before I feel I'm doing more harm than good, but—I tell my writing students this all the time—when you stop writing you're still writing!

Your subconscious does a lot of the work, and most of the best work. So, keep a pen and pad handy or some kind of recording device. Chances are you will keep having ideas even after you've put your work away for the day.

Q: What are the pros and cons of working as a staff writer?
A: One of the things, early on, that I think was very good for me, was the sense of responsibility to my publisher to be a disciplined writer, which is essential. I was blessed with great publishers pretty much throughout my career who, for the most part, let me go my own way, creatively. But having a publishing deal underlined the fact that songwriting is a job, and like all other jobs, you have to go to work whether you feel like it or not. You aren't going to get much done unless you sit your butt down every single day and do it.

Q: What do you like most about your job?
A: I feel incredibly lucky to have found a career that pays me to do what I would have done for free anyway. I'm a writer by nature, and would have been writing all my life regardless. But to be so richly rewarded for it (and not only in the literal sense) is something I didn't dare to dream about.

Q: What do you like least about your job?
A: I find writing excruciating. I don't find it "fun" at all. I get immense satisfaction from it, but it's hard, grueling work that comes with a motherlode of self-doubt about 90 percent of the time. That 10 percent of the time when things are magically flowing is the reward for the other 90 percent. And all of this is subjective. You never really know whether what you're working on is good or not. It's not like doing a math problem, where there's a right and a wrong answer. You have to learn to listen to your instincts.

Q: What personal qualities do you find most valuable for this type of work?
A: I've always thought my best asset was a really good set of blinders. When I hit the wall and can't seem to write, or go

through a period of debilitating self-doubt, or get a bad review, or receive anything that feels like a blow to the ego, I allow myself to wallow in it for a day or so and then I put the blinders on and go to work. I guess you might call that determination, but to me it really boils down to this: put your nose down and do your work. And you'll be in it for the long haul, and that in itself is something to be proud of.

Q: What advice do you have for students who might be interested in a career as a songwriter?
A: Make sure it's something you can't live without. Listen to feedback, but listen harder to your own gut. Honor the profession— you're not writing ad copy, you're describing the human condition. Rise to the occasion.

Q: What are your current songwriting projects?
A: In 2018 I released my latest solo album, *Dancing with the Beast,* which puts female characters at the fore, from teenage girls to old women. I'm currently working on an album of cover songs by my favorite songwriter, Mickey Newbury. Recording his songs is like taking a grad school course in songwriting.

Other Jobs in Music

A&R administrator

Audio engineer

Booking agent

Choreographer

Church choir director

Commercial jingle composer

Concert promotor

Conductor

Cruise ship performer

Dancer

Disc jockey

Entertainment attorney

Film composer

Foley artist

Front-of-house engineer

Instrument sales

Music arranger

Music curator

Music journalist

Music licensing administrator

Music teacher

Music therapist

Radio program director

Record producer

Recording engineer

Stage manager

Talent agent

Talent scout

Theater director

Tour manager

Editor's note: The US Department of Labor's Bureau of Labor Statistics provides information about hundreds of occupations. The agency's *Occupational Outlook Handbook* describes what these jobs entail, the work environment, education and skill requirements, pay, future outlook, and more. The *Occupational Outlook Handbook* may be accessed online at www.bls.gov/ooh.

Index

Picture Credits

About the Author

Stuart A. Kallen is the author of more than 350 nonfiction books for children and young adults. He has written on topics ranging from the theory of relativity to the art of electronic dance music. In 2018 Kallen won a Green Earth award from the Nature Generation environmental organization for his book *Trashing the Planet: Examining the Global Garbage Glut.* In his spare time he is a singer, songwriter, and guitarist in San Diego.